Poems for The Shepherd: A Heart longing for Him

Stacy Ferguson

BookLeaf Publishing

Presentation by *BookLeaf Publishing*

Web: www.bookleafpub.com

E-mail: info@bookleafpub.com

ISBN: 9789357696074

First edition 2023

DEDICATION

To my Moses

My friend, my love, my life.

I miss you and

I love you for always!

ACKNOWLEDGEMENT

I cannot begin to express my gratitude for my mom and my Grammy Ann. We Three is a blessing that I do not take for lightly. I am forever grateful that God gave me two amazing artists and writers, to not only influence and push me, but to grow me deep in the knowledge of my identity in Christ.

To say "thank you" to my husband is an understatement. What a precious gift and blessing you are to me. I love you more each day and I am forever grateful that you push me to love God deeper and stronger.

"Thank you" dad, Kenneth, Uncle Scott, Youngin and Savanna! I am forever grateful you believe in me and stand by me. God gave me the absolute epitome of family when He gave me you! You guys will forever have my heart.

I am forever indebted to my hero, Mr. Byrd. You are a divine appointment that I am forever and humbly grateful for. You believed in me in a way no one else ever has and always showed me Jesus. You gave me the courage to search and find my identity in Him. So, thank you for allowing God to use you in a young girl's life all those years ago and on into this day.

Bernie, when I asked God for a friend, I had no idea what He had in store. Thank you for showing me Jesus every day and taking me on adventures where I get to know Him better! Thank you for pouring into a crazy, complex, contradictory introvert. I am forever grateful for you!

I am so grateful to The Box and all that they have done for me from being a place to grow and disciple all the way to a place of support and security.

My second momma and daddy, you two are priceless and thank you will never be enough for all you have poured into my life and me since I was little!

Also, there are so many friends who show and share Jesus with me in so many ways and I am thankful to each and every one of you! He surrounded me with so many wonderful examples of warriors and words cannot express my gratitude!

Love,
Ferg
Numbers 6:24-26

PREFACE

"Oh God, you are my God, earnestly I seek you; my soul thirsts for you, my body longs for you..." Psalm 63:1

A prayer, a desk and a challenge.
The journey for seeking to find Jesus and walk in His dust is one that is constantly changing and full of grace. I long to know Him and look just like Him more and more every day. I want to be fully emersed in His dust and hear every single word His voice speaks.

This 21-day story begins with His name on my lips and ends with a heart more committed, more adoring and more refined than it started. Starting each morning in the presence of the Shepherd and pouring out what is stirring down in the depths of my heart, created an amazing adventure where I have experienced amazing growth in trusting Him.

Jesus

Just as my eyes open
Enters rays of brilliant light,
Son beams radiate,
Up on the serene mountain top
Shines the King of kings.

A Heart Longing to Trust

Aching to be covered in His dust
Anxious to be just one step closer
My ribs guard a heart longing to trust.

Hanging onto the moment, feeling like I must
Fight the walls and beat my fists against the glass
Aching to be covered in His dust.

A glass so thick if only I could bust
I see your smile, your eyes so full of grace
My ribs guard the ache of a heart longing to trust.

I see you speak, the words, my ears yearning to adjust
A crack in the glass, all I know to do is fight
Aching to be covered in His dust.

This prison I am trapped in, closed and unjust
My fight is gone, and the exhaustion overtakes
My ribs guard the ache of a heart longing to trust.

A lifeless heart falling into the arms of the one that is
just
He holds me close under His wings with a fight won
Aching to be covered in His dust,
My ribs guard the ache of a heart longing to trust.

Light of the Night

My eyes begin to open, scared to hope
The cloud of darkness breaking
My soul desperate to cope;

I look to the sky,
The stars whisper of a hope to be found
My heart longs to find;

A tear sneaks down my cheek
As the moon radiates its light
I want to hear You speak,

All my heart dreams of, all the love I could find;
I know You hold it in Your hand as You reach to hold mine.

Conquer the Storm

Crack of the fire, peace in the dark
A single light, as you speak to my heart.
Known and adored covered in grace,
As the new dawn rises staying in Your embrace.

Light peeks through the window panes,
Darkness scatters as it begins to rain.
Grace and mercy fill every part
Your feathers covering every piece of my heart,

The thunder echoes as the rain pours;
The light piercing the darkness as I continue to look
for
Peace and rest to fall on me,
Looking to You, You are the only one I see.

The storm rages as the promise of victory is coming,
A rainbow breaks through, the one true King is
stunning!

Invisible

Faces rush by day after day
Each with their own look
Some searching you
Some questioning you
And still others judging you;

Never giving you the chance
To show what is deep inside
Never taking a split second
Just to listen to your side.

What burns in your heart to be said
They selfishly talk and judge
Taking all you can possibly give,
Till they pass another unsuspecting face
How much more can one give
To a world with no grace?

I do not know
I can't possibly understand
The Word becoming human
Constricted to the flesh and bone
And laying down life for a world of takers
Loving each and every one He calls known.

They may pass,
They may judge,
But there is One that doesn't care what this world
thinks
He simply walks and searches for a heart that is
Never seen, but lies in the invisible!

This is My Desire

This is my desire
my heart yearning

A journey to hear Him
A journey to know Him

My only desire
The one thing I need

Is all of Him
Holding all of me!

Known

8

Knowing you hold the darkest part
Never letting go, never truly falling apart;
Over and over, You draw me close
When I'm unaware I need it most,
Name above all names!

Trapped in Time

The heart fights the mortality of the flesh knowing it
was truly made for more
Then a fleeting moment.

How do you fight the wisdom of an eternal bound
heart when the physical
World is held captive by time?

Freed?

The beast rages, beating on the cage of my heart
I feel him begging, "Let me tear you apart!"
The ache in my chest
Growing stronger each day
Begging me, "Please, just let me have my way!"

The triggers, so many, no matter what I do
I'm holding on
To the only One who's true!
You have the key the only thing I need
Please lock him up
NEVER to be freed.

Answer the Knock

The cold sweeps through the night
My eyes desperate to open,
I hear You whisper
The knock at the door;

My heart is willing but
My flesh is so weak,
I lay there begging
knowing I simply cannot walk the path;

I want to, I really do
The cold heavy on my chest,
an ache in my bones
My soul longs to move towards you.

Hours turn the night into day
And the cold releases
I'm late,
Oh, forgive my heart,
but here I am

The door now open
I'm all yours in this moment!

Wrapped in Your Depths

Jesus,
This is so heavy,
I can't see who You say I am.
The sinking in my heart
Knowing the darkness of my heart;

I want to know Your love-
I want to be wrapped in the depths-
I want to see how wide and long and high and deep,
Hold me in Your arms and whisper Your truth;

The cold creeping in, begging me to see
All the imperfections,
You knock beckoning me,
Speaking-
To my soul to be set free;

In the depths of Your love,
To be covered with the waves of the deep
To feel the love, You have for me
I want to live in Your truth,
Wrapped tightly in Your love!

His Disciple

Loving my Jesus
The truth He holds can be found
Walking in His dust

Mold Me

The human experience is nothing less than shattering!
A life we never got to hold
A piece of our story a memory often forgotten
Left our hearts so cold.

Robbed of a future,
A presence stolen.
Hard is never fair
And it always leaves all things broken.

The flesh of my bones aches
And mourns,
The loss of a heart, I never got to hold.
Teach me to walk through the hard
Make my heart like Yours!
BOLD!

Oh! My Jesus

Oh! Jesus, my Shepherd
Always walking through the valleys
    and on the mountain tops with me
    tender, loving and faithful
I long to follow on.

Oh! Jesus, my Savior
   Willingly laying down your life
   to save even just one that is lost
You are so merciful
You take my breath away.

Oh! Jesus my King
   Making all things new
   Mighty, perfect and Holy.

Not even the ends of the universe can compare to
You!

11/15

Let us live today to honor her name
as You tenderly watch her in Heaven,
Allow her infectious giggle to echo through the
clouds
to ring to the deepest joys of Your love
As You hold her in Your arms.

Thank You for holding our girl,
Help us to seek every moment with the joy,
The joy I know that radiates from her smile.

Today is Your day, Lord!
Sing over her!
As You celebrate the day she walked home to You!

A Nonet

The darkness rising and night threatens
Clouds build and coldness fills the air
He whispers to the broken
The storm breaks and rain falls
I rush to His arms
Held in His grace
My Savior
Jesus
King

Dancing

The crisp morning air stings as it tickles my skin,
The morning beams rising as the clouds dance,
Waves crash against the tender sand and
New mercy rains down over me.

Covering a heart torn and beaten,
Grace fills every hurt,
My eyes look up to the Heavens
As grace smiles down over me.

His hand waiting as the sun leaps off the waters,
A moment of hope,
My eyes alive and bright as I reach for Him,
He wraps me in His arms and carries me down the
beach.

A small giggle escapes my lips
As He dances down the beach
My weakest hurt and deepest brokenness,
And He carries it all dancing;
Dancing down the beach!

His Voice

Speaks tenderly
Faithfully, mercifully, gracefully
Words whispered

Calling

Whispered words
Gracefully, mercifully,faithfully
Tenderly speaks

Your Love

The rain falls
As the dawn stalls,
Clouds threaten
As the storm settles in.

A wave of ache
This heart about to break,
As the tears fall
Your voice gently calls.

The lightning flashes
And thunder clashes,
I run to you
Mercy falls brand new.

Each year falls like rain
I'll never be the same,
You carry me
You're all I want to see.

How great is Your love;
How great is Your love!

Victory

The ache of breath beneath my ribs
The star's desperation for the night;

My hopes sailing on the waves of grief
As the moon fills the sky with light;

Grace washing over me in the depths
Clouds filling the air blinding my sight;

Sadness overwhelms as my thoughts drop anchor
The thunder crashes as lighting blazes white;

A flood of broken runs down my face
The storm echoes the threat to hold tight;

The beaten heart foreshadows His victory
The wind hints through the leaves all that is right;

The cracks of brokenness filled with grace on end
A rainbow flashes as His love covers to win this
FIGHT!

A Warrior

A heart of a warrior
   Battered and bruised
The grace of the King
   Tender and true.

You hold my heart
   Hard and cold
Please make me like You
   Graceful and bold.

Covered in Your dust
   Loyal and adored
Molded by the Victor
   Tried and endured.

A table set
   Remember and see
The King sits down just
   You and me.

A heart longing deeply
   Mold and refine
A Shepherd whispers
   You are all mine!